TRUTH MUST BE TOLD

Goddess Ravin Nicole

TABLE OF CONTENTS

Psychological Warfare-pg1

Gate-Keepers-pg7

The Media-pg13

Chemical Warfare-pg15

Spiritual Warfare-pg22

Emotional/Energy Warfare-pg28

Mental Enslavement-pg33

Hidden Knowledge-pg40

Christ Consciousness-pg44

Inner-World-pg51

Outer-World-pg57

Natal Chart/Birth Chart-pg61

Realms/Dimensions/Timelines-pg65

Chakras-pg70

Crystals-pg76

Word Alchemy-pg79

I DARE YOU TO CHALLENGE YOURSELF BY CHALLENGING YOUR WORLD-VIEW.

-GODDESS RAVIN NICOLE

Psychological Warfare

Look up this patent number on google or whichever search engine you use: US6506148B2, this will show you that they are using tel-lie-vision to manipulate the masses nervous system.

This physiological manipulation influences people's thoughts, emotions, and behavior. They know that people pay more attention to sensational information and respond to stimulation that has a weak electromagnetic field and low frequencies, effortlessly.

They know that it excites a sensory resonance and when showing pulsated images, which emits pulsed electromagnetic fields and with enough amplitudes will cause physiological arousal within someone. Which makes it possible for them to input whatever they want into people's minds using certain images displaying through these black boxes (tel-lie-vision and monitors, aka surveillance, because most of all TVs have built-in cameras), to manipulate them and plant ideas in their minds.

So, people are being brainwashed, surveilled, and their emotions are being manipulated, and their reality is being manufactured for them. They are also being desensitized and manipulated to behave, act, and think in a particular way. They are controlled, lost, and under a spell. And they are easily programmed and controlled by constantly tuning in to all these low-vibrational frequencies. Which have a long-term aim and effect on their psyche and their emotional well-being.

Even playing violent video games can have a detrimental effect on a person's psyche. See, when people are consuming these low vibrational frequencies their emotions and mental are being manipulated and toyed with.

And there are subliminal messages in the forefront and background of these games and programs (that the subconscious mind picks up on and stores that information), that is socially engineering people. Especially, the youth to harm, kill, and destroy their own reflections. See, you have to over-stand that the nervous system controls everything in the body and the brain.

Nerves and cells carry messages to and from the brain and the spinal cord to different parts of the body. So, if someone (ex: child or adult) is sitting watching programs with violence, sex, drugs, and killing or even playing it in a video game.

What do you think their mental, emotional, or physical response is going to be in real life situations, especially in fight or flight mode? When a person is constantly being manipulated and influenced through the tel-lie-vision and game console (con-sole/deceiving your soul).

And every year they do the Black Friday, and people are out here trying to buy the biggest tel-lie-vision helping with their own demise and watching programs that shows them behaving and acting in a negative manner on a lower frequency.

And that is what you call Psychological Warfare. People's behavior, actions, thoughts, emotions, and perception is being influenced and manipulated, constantly and inured to violence.

Not to mention, the liquor stores, drug dealers, and churches on every corner in oppressed and suppressed neighborhoods keeping the people from growing and evolving mentally, emotionally, spiritually, and physically. Now we see why there is so much, so called black on black crimes that happens in our communities or in a community near you. Because it's systematically done, and we are being inundated with low frequencies and negative imagery, each and everywhere we turn or look.

Even the music industry system and your favorite artist, promotes crime and serial killing music against your own reflections. Or sexual inappropriate behavior. It's like animal conditioning and one of their biggest weapons they use against the masses. Like why and how is this okay, and accepted within our reality and our society. But I guess without the promotion of negativity and things that have negative influential effect on our mind and behavior there will be no crimes, and this beast system cannot uphold itself without people being docile and ignorant and participating in their own self-destruction.

So, it continues to keep the masses from knowing who they truly are and behaving worse than animals. Because, if you ever come into the realization and awareness of who you are, their whole beast system will crumble. Therefore, the fake powers that be will continue to do anything to keep you distracted from knowing thy-self and the powerful being you truly are and the inner and outer power you deeply hold within all this chaos and destruction.

And that is what you call psychological warfare. It is a war against your mind and spirit. And you must release these disempowering programs and become whole within.

<u>GATE-KEEPERS</u>

A lot of people have sold and lost their soul to this system for a false sense of power, control, and material gains. Or because they are oblivious to what is going on around them. But many of them do know and they are the gatekeepers, put in place to keep you docile and trapped, in a cycle of self-destruction and illusions.

The gatekeepers will give you half-truths but never the whole truth. Which in return corrupts your beliefs, understanding, perception, and influence your decisions and control your actions. And this is a highly effective, dangerous tactic that they use to control and manipulate you. They do not want to lose their false sense of power and control. Or their homes, cars, and vacation days. Or their government funding and government contracts.

Especially, those that could make a difference but their status in the community, job title, high pay brackets, and government contracts, etc., that they are tied to, forbids them to do so. So, they will turn a blind eye, instead of speaking the whole truth.

While assisting in keeping you caught up in the same internal and external mental constraints and restraints. And other illusions that keep you time-looping in the same scenarios, experiences, programs, and cycles. That gives you a false sense of hope, power, and control (ex: voting rights, community programs, jobs, money, etc.). That will never unchain your mind.

Even these pastors are gatekeepers cause they know the truth but will never tell you the depths of this and that either. Or how religion keeps you trapped in a cycle of feeling powerless, despair, and emotional distress. Or in a repetitive pattern of feeling stuck, with a loss of sense of self and hope, while waiting on a savior outside of yourself to rescue you. When only you can save yourself.

Maybe the reason they do not speak the truth to help you free your mind and save yourself. Has something to do with the tithes you pay them or the feeling of power and control they have over you. Or their superiority complex they feel having you believing thou is holier than you. By having you thinking that you need a middleman to connect to the Divine Mother and Father.

Or it's their subsidy from the govern-ment the 501C3 voucher they receive that exempts them from paying taxes on the tithes you give them. Or because they are soldiers for the beast or all the above. They do go hand in hand.

So, be careful and use your discernment when you get caught up in these systems (ex: churches, jail, jobs) and meet people that look like you and you start to think because you share the same skin tone that they are for you. All skin-folks are not kinfolks. They are gatekeepers for these community programs and rehabilitation programs, etc., and they do not have your best interest at heart.

Because if they did, they will teach and show you how to confide and trust in yourself and your own abilities. Instead of keeping your inner knowing suppressed. And they would tell you the reasons why you are, the way you are. And how things are orchestrated and done by design, to keep you suppressed and oppressed. By keeping you stuck on the hamster wheel going in circles, while depending on someone outside of yourself to save you.

Also, keep in mind that the people that are controlling

them sends them, to keep you in control. And they will never give

you the knowledge that will free your mind.

If they were for you, they would tell you the truth, and

nothing but the truth. But they will never, because they love and

protect the system that keeps your mind trapped, and them

comfortable and paid.

And without conditioned, brainwashed people that commit

crimes of violence. Or those that do not know their ass from their

asshole. Their jobs and titles will cease to exist, and their money

will stop. Therefore, they will never give you the knowledge to

liberate yourself. So, stay mindful because they are dangerous.

Furthermore, back in our ancestors' days they were known

as "Sambo's," not "Uncle Tom's." There is a misconception in

today society that the Uncle Tom's, were and are the traitors, when in all actuality, it is the Sambos, that were and are the

traitor's aka Gatekeepers. In addition, gatekeepers come in all

sizes and colors. So do not ever be confused thinking they only

look like you.

THE MEDIA

The media is a broadcast system. Now, think about that for a second. Broad is a mass of people. That are watching and tuning in to the programming. Or the targeted audience. And casting is to cast a magic spell, or something that is being directed in a certain direction.

Now that I have simplified that down, let us put it all together. They are broadcasting spells onto a scope or large amount of people that are tuning in, watching, and channeling the energy/entities that the frequency of the broadcast is emitting. Which could be fear, depression, grief, violence, tragedy, suffering, sickness, illness, sadness, addictions, or sexually explicit behavior. So, they are deceiving and tricking your senses.

These are psychological tactics/weapons or dark spiritual practices used to control you, confuse you, tear you down, wear your spirit down, and separate you from yourself, and the Divine Spirit. The media main usage is to program your mind, spread fear, and cast illusionary spells, *hear me now*. They are spreading fear, propaganda, playing on your emotions, and directing your energy, and mind in the direction they want it to go. And remember, they do this with misleading information, violence, drugs, money, and sexually explicit content through the tel-lie-vision, social media, and any other media outlets, as well as the game con-sole system.

Chemical Warfare

The food is poisonous; the pharmaceutical drugs are poisonous. The fluoride water is poisonous, and the air quality is poisonous. And there are dangerous chemicals in the food in these fast-food restaurants. That is why they are all over the communities in which you live.

Several known dangerous chemicals contained in fast food are calcium sulfate, propylene glycol, dimethylpolysiloxane, butylated hydroxyanisole/hydroxytoluene, and potassium bromate. And these chemicals cause severe health risks to the body. That is why people have obesity, diabetes, high cholesterol, and heart problems, etc. People are falling sick and are dying from these harsh chemicals.

TRUTH MUST BE TOLD

And the food that is natural and healthy for you such as fruits and vegetables are now bioengineered or made seedless. Oh, and let's not forget the 3D printed meat that is now in circulation. And the food in impoverished communities stores are highly processed food and is GMOs (genetically modified organisms), and it's all done by design. They know people in these areas lack reliable transportation to stores where naturally grown food is sold or they are on a limited budget, so they will purchase this hazardous food in order to eat and feed their family.

This is called Chemical Warfare. So, it is in your best interest to start to grow your own food or buy from farmers that you know are selling naturally grown food that has not been produced and added with harmful chemicals. Not only is these chemicals harmful for you they are also suppressing your spiritual awakening.

Now, let discuss the evil sorcerer's are should I say the big pharma's and the scientist's that practice medicine and give you these synthetic drugs, and lethal, detrimental, vaccinations. They only give you drugs that suppress your symptoms, but they do not provide you the cure for any dis-eases or viruses.

These evil sorcerers will never tell or give you the cure for your dis-eases, because they will go out of business. There will be no pharmacies or hospitals if they cured you. So, they don't focus on the spiritual or psychological genesis aspects of the illness or dis-ease, but only the mechanical treatment of symptoms but never the prevention or cure. So, they not going to tell you that there's a natural plant you could take to permanently get rid of known dis-eases or illnesses, along with eating healthier. Ask your drug pusher, I mean; Doctor, is it true that there are natural plants for all dis-eases or illnesses that will cure sick people. It is known as holistic healing.

See, you have to over-stand that when people have dis-eases or some sort of illness, it is usually an ailment through which the body is expressing that something is out of alignment within them.

For example, when there is an imbalance in your root chakra it can affect your immune system, etc. An imbalance heart chakra can cause heart dis-eases or respiratory issues or malfunctions.

But keep in mind that the body can naturally heal itself or there is a natural plant that can. Also, certain healing frequencies can heal different body parts as well. Or just simply, changing your diet can help you heal and live a longer and healthier life.

Moving along, the water supply in impoverished communities is laced with fluoride which calcifies your pineal gland aka third eye. And a calcified pineal gland keeps you from having clarity, spiritual discernment, connecting to your higher-self, higher dimensions, higher consciousness, your ancestors, your angels, and the Divine. Or from tapping in and developing your clairvoyance powers, which is clear seeing.

See, your pineal gland is your sixth chakra, and it is where you experience your clairvoyance. It is located between your anatomical eyes. And it is the most heavily targeted and poisoned organ in the body.

Due to its spiritual intelligence and the influence, it has on your awareness, creativity, imagination, consciousness, inner wisdom, and spiritual insight that goes beyond physical

TRUTH MUST BE TOLD

perception. See, a calcified pineal gland means your mind can easily be deceived.

But a decalcified pineal gland acts as a truth detector and can notice subtle anomalies and inconsistencies, lies, or subliminal messages that are used as veils to conceal the truth or real intentions of people.

So filtered water and avoiding processed foods and fluoride free toothpaste or meditating are some of the few things you can do to assist with decalcifying your pineal gland.

And you may already know how they use alcohol, lab grown marijuana, and other synthetic drugs and street drugs to cause a negative impact to the third eye and body. So, listen here, chemical and biological warfare is not a game and should be taken very seriously.

P a g e | 20

Now, moving along, go outside and look up. Do you see the chemtrails shooting from certain aircrafts? There are toxic chemicals in those chemtrails that are sprayed through your skies daily. These chemicals cause infections, sterilization, reduction of life expectancy, mind control, weather control, and cloud seeding, etc. They are poisoning you mentally, emotionally, physically, and spiritually daily. Silent weapons for quiet wars.

Spiritual Warfare

Spiritual Warfare is real, and it is not a metaphor or symbolic language for emotional struggle. It is real and it operates in dimensions that the natural eyes cannot see. And it has been going on for eons. And the seen and unseen malevolent, negative, demonic, opposing forces are real. Dark magic and witchcraft are real. Witches and warlocks are real. People doing dark magic and casting spells on you is real. Depression, mental illness, stress, addiction, suicide, anxiety, and fear, etc., is an unclean, binding, evil, malevolent spirit and it's real.

Getting attacked by lower vibrational entities is real. Being persuaded and controlled by thoughts that are not your own is real. Being manipulated, abused, and lied on, is sorcery, and it's real. Fighting and battling evil dark forces that are coming up against you is real. Having these demonic negative forces on your job or in your family, as parents, spouses, or friends, is real.

When you are out living in the dark and unrighteously, these evil forces can easily attack you. Especially, when you vibrate on their lower frequencies; you are playing in the devil's playground. Where that evil force and its minion are in control and will gain power over you and destroy you.

They are evil, deceptive, and destructive. If you are not aware of these dark forces, and an easy target, they can and will manipulate, dominate, control, and take over you. So, you must be aware, careful, and covered in the Divine Spirit, *armor.* Because they are out here lurking and waiting to possess those vessels that do not know thy-self, or that are not in tune with energy. And aren't aware of what or who these energies/spirits are or how they operate.

Even if you are living for the Divine Spirit, and righteously, these evil forces will still try to attack you, try to rob you of your light, joy, and peace. Or it will tempt you or get you to do something you wouldn't normally do.

They know you are a child of the Divine Spirit, and they see your light and they know that you are here on assignment. With the purpose of fulfilling your mission and/or to break generational curses, that are within your family bloodline, and they do not like it. Your light shines brightly and reflects on others inner and outer demons. And they know that you are the truth and you have come to speak the truth.

They are terrified and do not want you to discover who you are or walking in your purpose and knowing that you are more powerful than the demonic entity that is trying to knock you down. These unseen forces can astral project into your dreams to try to create chaos within you or your awakening state. Or they will try to attach themselves to you. They want your reality distorted and full of confusion. But what they really want aside from taking over your vessel and tainting your spirit, or having you lose your soul, is to come against your mind, your peace, your purpose, your destiny, and soul mission.

The way to keep yourself protected from these negative energies is to fight back and block and stay away from anyone that has malicious and ill intent for your life. Use spiritual discernment and move accordingly, set boundaries, stay aligned in higher frequencies, keep your energy, vibration, and thoughts positive. Especially, when encountering these low vibrating entities. Cause energy is contagious and transferable, so stay positive in the midst of it all.

Because they will try to attack your mind, body, and spirit. And these negative forces can become obsessed with you and your energy and will do anything to bring you down to their level.

Because they know they can only severely attack you, if they can get you to drop your frequency and vibration and get you out of alignment and down to the lower frequencies that they dwell and are experts in. They will also try to trigger you that's why healing is so important. And they will try to have you thinking low vibratory thoughts to try to get you to operate on a lower vibrational frequency.

But if you know your own energy and how you think, feel, and act. Then your intuition and body will alert you when something is off and out of alignment and/or if you have been in contact with one of these evil forces. And the Divine Spirit will always protect you and shield you from these negative forces.

Just make sure you are living right and not out here entertaining demons or being amongst the wicked. Because them lessons only gets harder when you are.

Energy/Emotional Warfare

Energy/Emotional warfare and parasitic energy is real, and it exist in this physical, material, earthly realm that we live in. This energy is always doing things to feed off your energy and emotions. They feed off your downfall, your grief, trauma, pain, sadness, anger, misfortune, and fear etc. They feed off the emotions that are low in frequency.

It is always trying to drain and deplete you of your vitality and to cause you some form of dire circumstances or situations. That will have you stressed out, exhausted, and worn out, without any strength left in your being, physically or mentally, etc.,. So, it can be able to feed off your loosh. Loosh aka Chi, is your essence, it is your life force energy that is within you and all around you. It can also be an emotional energy that radiates from fear or severe suffering in the mind and body.

And it's a desired fuel/food source for these entities. They do not like the loosh you radiate from being kind, empathetic, fulfilled, grounded, grateful, compassionate, positive, happy, joyful, balanced, or inner peace. That god-like energy.

No, they need that energy that is stored in your body or mental from unresolved trauma. And they will use different tactics to trigger those emotions and wounds within you.

For example, through the tel-lie-vision. That is why they are always displaying negative depictive images of violence, grief, pain, suffering, and sorrow, of your reflections on that tel-lie-vision. Or announcing negative information through their news or radio to drag your emotions and vibration down.

Even rage, anger or ruthless energy can fuel and empower this energy. It can feed off any negative forms of energy. That's why it's always trying to keep you operating from your root chakra instead of your heart and crown chakras.

The root chakra is located at the base of your spine. And when it's blocked or in an imbalance state it has scattered energies and has you in fear, insecure, unstable, ungrounded, and with low physical energy etc.

If you pay close attention, you will start to see the different form of energies that feed off your Chi. This energy likes to attach itself to a host and most of the time it's someone close to you that has already been body snatched and can transfer this energy onto you. Or you can do it to yourself from vibrating low and subscribing to negativity. This energy can also jump hosts very rapidly like in a blink of an eye. Watch the movie Fallen with

Denzel Washington, it shows you how this energy can jump into different hosts.

And it does things to antagonize you to put you in these lower states. Some people already carry this energy signature. Those that are known as Jezebel's, Judas' or Leviathan's, and narcissist's, these energies operate in chaos, confusion and destruction.

Or the drunken energy that is very toxic and chaotic. It use these energies as a host to lower your vibration and feed off your energy. It's a must when you notice these energies around you to get far away because it comes to bring destruction to anyone on its path. And it's vital that you over-stand that these lower emotions and lower vibrations isn't your natural state. These opposing, negative forces that I mentioned above are actively working to keep the collective consciousness in a lower frequency so they can feed off you. They are playing a subtle yet powerful game of manipulation and deceit. Yet, they are not the ultimate power. You have the ability to transcend these lower emotions, vibrations, and frequencies, and ascend to higher states of consciousness that are always within your reach.

<u>Mental Enslavement</u>

Mental enslavement has disempowered, overpowered, and mentally chained our society. There are free thinkers who try to get the masses to question their existence and reality, but they are shunned, ostracized, and called conspiracy theorists.

They first started by trying to warn their family members but were called crazy and delusional. So, they tried taking the information they know and teach it to the masses to warn them of the mental imprisonment and indoctrination that is going on, but everyone is so blinded by mind control and can't see past the disguises that are hidden in plain sight.

No one wants to see the pollution that has taken over their mind and how they are under mind control and being mentally programmed. And how they have been conditioned to the lowest form on the totem pole.

They are in bondage, psychologically locked down and do not even realize it or care enough to change their circumstances and free themselves. They continue to hurt themselves and others while suffering internally, instead of healing and choosing life and saving their soul.

This programming started at an early age. The brainwashing and indoctrination of the young minds of children that have now become adults. And the cycle repeats and becomes a generational curse.

A child before the age of seven is easier to program and indoctrinate with lies and illusions. And if the parents do not know or do better, they will assist with the mental genocidal destruction of their own child, their self-image, and culture, by following the beast program. It is not the Divine they are serving i is the system of the beast.

We are not born with sins, but we are born into a world full of sins. Sending children to these school institutions to be indoctrinated and that do not allow the child to critically think for themselves is what most parents do to their children. Because they are too lazy and mentally disturbed to teach their own offsprings. Or because the beast machine keeps them so busy and distracted, which in return gives them no time or means to teach their own offsprings.

However, you will never see in nature a lion or lioness letting a hyena raise and teach their offsprings. Or a honeybee trying to be a fly.

If you bring up a child the way you want them to go, they will never detour from the path, according to the good book. The mind of a child is fragile and easy to program in its early development stage.

So, teaching a child to accept and conform to lies, knowing no Easter bunny lay eggs, leaves no room for critical thinking and intellect. And lying to the children is teaching and showing them it's okay to lie because you're lying to them about made up stuff and teaching them that they cannot trust you. And the one thing that always gets me going is telling your children there is a big, fat, pale face man in a red suit, riding on a sled of reindeers delivering presents to obedient children in one night.

And that's just preposterous. Just tell the truth you done slave to a system to get those presents. Probably, behinds on bills and on the verge of getting evicted for upholding the lie. Instead of telling the truth or not participating in the mental genocide of these holidays. Why fall victim to following societal-destruction.

Teaching your child a pale face man in the sky floating on a white cloud is watching and one day sending his pale face son back to save them all, from the pale face oppressors. While

grandma got his picture hanging from the wall in the front hall

knowing he looks nothing like them. And the same depicted

image is in the churches.

No resemblance, whatsoever. And the man on the Quaker

Oats box must be the big man himself giving you your daily bread.

This is absurd and out of control.

If you believe and participate in this system of

destruction and uphold the lies, then the curses shall remain. And

until you all start facing reality instead of being afraid to do so,

the programming and mental enslavement will continue to be

passed down generation after generation.

If only you knew the real history of these holidays and

other things, such as these different systems that keeps your

mind locked down. You wouldn't even make a fool out of yourself by participating in all the foolery. Self-hate is real and if you're not taking accountability for your actions and instilling the right programs and images in your children's minds, and the truth of all matters, then the destruction will continue generation after generation.

Learn to believe and trust in yourself and your own inner knowing. Be kind to yourself and love yourself, and your reflections, teach your young ones to do the same and to think for themselves. And to seek knowledge, wisdom, and inner-standing in everything that they do.

Teach them their roots and how great they are and how great their ancestors were, and how great we are and were together. Pour into them and teach them that the great Divine Spirit is within them and is always watching over them and keeping them protected along with their ancestors, angels, and spiritual team. Raise them to be fearless, with the knowledge of knowing themselves. This is valuable information, pay attention.

Tell them how they can be anything they put their mind, time, energy, and creativity to. If not, someone else will use their mind, time, energy, and creativity to build the world they want. Which mentally entraps them deeper into a system that is built to keep them shameful, stuck, lost, and self-destructing.

Meanwhile, this system also keeps them chasing after money, material gains, clout, attention, and validation, which is usually short-lived, serving only as a temporary fix for the internal pain and loss they feel within.

Consequently, the cycles keeps repeating generation after generation. Until someone is brave and bold enough to come forth and put an end to it all.

Hidden Knowledge

Esoteric, metaphysics, and occult, (which means hidden) knowledge transcends conventional beliefs and modern mundane human perception. Society as which you know has been conditioned to reject deeper knowledge and anything outside of their comfort zones and beliefs. So, their mental barriers of resistance (Agent Smith's) often kicks in and prevents them from exploring the possibility that a vast of unseen energetic realities (that influence the physical world), exist and can be observed. Or that multiple dimensions exists outside of their level of consciousness or awareness, simultaneously, with their own dimension. But a spiritual awakening, deep studying, or heighten awareness is needed to bypass their psychological blocks, in order to have this kind of knowledge, power, or the ability to perceive, receive, or observe, and understand supernatural or paranormal energies that are outside of this third-dimensional construct and its programs.

Also, with this awareness/consciousness of unseen energy forces that is other-worldly and transcendent, can also be observed through extrasensory perception, such as having the gift of clairsentience (clear feeling), or clairvoyance (clear seeing), or clairaudience (clear hearing), or claircognizance (clear knowing), to name just a few. Or having a level of awareness/consciousness on how these energies operate. And having this supernatural awareness or sensitivity to unseen energies places you on a spiritual level of awareness, or the dimensional frequency of the energies. And the knowing of these energies will allow you to obtain and retain information through mystical means, while simultaneously seeing through the invisible veil that keeps you stuck in lower states of consciousness. But you will be able to break through the illusions (sometimes called maya) using your spiritual eye, also known as the first eye or third eye.

This is your spiritual sight which gives you spiritual insight, discernment, and the ability to perceive and see the true world, not the mundane reality or false images that were initially presented and programmed into you. You begin to see things as they truly are. Including, the shapeshifters that live among us. You will be able to see and sense other energies or entities that tries to attach themselves to you or that is giving you a message (there are higher benevolent beings as well as malevolent). And you'll be able to see spirits, angels, or demons, whose images or energies are hidden from others. This can be very hard to comprehend and grasp, and you may feel a little skeptical at first. But once you tap into self, you'll see it's like water to a dolphin.

Secret hidden knowledge, energies, hidden dimensions, spiritual truths, inner knowing, is all enlightenment and only available to those who dare to color outside the lines of the collective consciousness. All these things can help you reach some level of enlightenment and/or inner transformation, self-mastery, spiritual enlightenment, self-empowerment, and elevate you to a higher state of consciousness and awareness.

Such as the Kybalion, sacred geometry, the flower of life, the tree of life, Gnosticism, esoterism, occultism, metaphysics, alchemy, transmutation, manifestation, astrology, numerology, meditation, yoga, etc., and knowing energies and how they operate and how to transmute them is good for your personal development and betterment.

Christ Consciousness

Christ consciousness, commonly known as Jesus, is a ENERGY and the epitome of the Divine Light. When Jesus said that he will return, he was speaking about the energy that will return to this earthly realm. See, Jesus, knew the people were asleep and under a spell, and had spiritual blindness. But he also knew this energy would return and the people would start to have spiritual awakenings, inner-transformations, and healing powers, that aligned with this energy. See, your salvation depends on you and is within you. No one, I repeat, No one is coming to save you. Only you can save you, nothing external of you can truly save you; it starts and ends with you. The internal process of your inner-transformations and spiritual awakenings is all you. Only you can choose to heal and deliver yourself from mental anguish and the beast system and its way of being. And only you can choose to live righteously; no one else can do it for you. Your Divinity, Christ Consciousness, and the Kingdom of Heaven lies within you.

Also, some people on this earthly realm already naturally, hold this Christ-like energy signature and walks amongst us. However, they are in this world but not of it. And whoever seeks or wishes to tap into this energy and heal and activate their heart chakra and elevate to Christ consciousness will have the free will to do so and be illuminated.

See, when Christ Consciousness was on the earth, it was pure, powerful, peaceful, miraculous, healing, intentional, creative, innovative, fearless, and the living truth.

It was free-spirited, compassionate, kind, loving, and a harmonious and balanced energy that could be felt by those in tune. And we all have the power and ability to be and do as such.

But it requires getting rid of old and out-dated belief systems that have indoctrinated you to believe that a savior outside of yourself is coming to save you. Letting go and releasing any constraints or restraints that limits you and keep you from moving inward and *internally* transforming. Because only you can save yourself by healing, changing, and turning from your wicked ways and walking in this Christ-like energy.

So, you must go within and heal and activate your heart chakra and Christ consciousness also known as the crown chakra. Healing requires you to get to the roots of your trauma by releasing and healing the pain, which likely stems from your childhood.

So, you must do the inner-child healing and the shadow work by going deep within. Sitting with yourself and asking yourself questions like why do I operate and behave the way I do, or why do I feel this way. Etc.,. These are questions you'll need to ask yourself. Because it's all about inner-child healing and shadow work and getting to the root of your problems. So, heal the root so the tree is stable.

And it is your birthright to be in alignment with Christ Consciousness.

But you must do the work and stop thinking someone outside of yourself can do it for you or is coming to save you. No one is coming, and you already have the tools within you to save yourself.

See, when The Divine Spirit, was talking to Moses and told him that, he *already* had the tools he needed to free the people out of Egypt, and from the hands of Pharaoh.

So, you see, Moses already had what he needed. The Divine Spirit was with him and was guiding and leading him along his path. And he had everything he needed within him. So, when you start to heal, the Divine is with you, and in you, and guiding you, and have already given you the tools you will need to succeed along your path on each level you elevate up to (consciously).

Also, Jesus, even mentions in John 14:6 that the only way to the Divine is through me. And that it is the truth and the light.

Meaning, the only way back to source is going within yourself and operating from the heart space like a child with a heart light as a feather and from your Christ Consciousness, while walking in your truth, your Divine power, and Divine light and being your true, healed, authentic self. He also said in John 14:12 that greater work you will do than him...by believing in him (By believing in yourself). So, he was mirroring back to you who you are on a soul level or at the core of your being (So, you could re-member who you are, his teaching wasn't about obedience but how to activate your own divinity that is within you), and trying to

show you how to awaken from the illusion (He was breaking

spells that was put on the masses, that's why they hung him), and

access the Divine directly and step outside the control and fear

system.

In conclusion, as you begin to heal, you will start to vibrate out

of your lower nature and away from people of a lower vibration,

that is not a vibrational match as your own. Your mind will begin

to alter from that beast consciousness and to the epitome of the

Christ consciousness. And what you once were accustomed to or

accepted and tolerated, all those low vibrational negative

energies and frequencies will begin to be repelled by your Christ

Consciousness and high vibrations. And there will be challenges

along the way, but you can overcome them. And know that these

challenges that you will face is building your temple/character, strength, power, resilience, and determination within you. So,

embrace these challenges with optimism because they are

opportunities for self-mastery. Crown on!!!

Inner-World

The inner-world is your world. The world inside of you. The spark of life that is within, your essence, your energy signature aka your spirit, this is the essence of who you are at heart.

It is where the Kingdom of Heaven and all your gifts, creativity, magic, ideas, talents, and Divine purpose reside. It's where all your thoughts, inner-dialogue, emotions, and feelings are. And where your hidden wounds and traumas are stored. And where your past and current memory bank is stored.

It's what's within you that creates your outer-world reality. Whatever is going on within you will reflect back to you in your outer-world, the good and the bad. Most don't know this information and wreak havoc in their own life, then blame a force outside of themselves that's creating the misery in which they live.

When no one has more power and control over your life than you do. Yes, outside forces can try to manipulate your life, but you have the power within you to change or stop anything coming up against you.

But if you are not aware of this, you give your power away freely. And trust that there are people out there that will love to control and dominate your life. Because it makes them feel empowered, which compensates for their lack of control and discipline over their own life, and their lack of sense of self, and their internal emptiness.

However, let's continue, if thoughts, emotions, and beliefs create reality, then it's important that you build solid foundations be intentional with your thoughts, how you feel, your beliefs, and what you want to create for yourself.

So, be mindful of your thoughts and feelings because they will manifest into your outer-world and play a part in your reality.

For example, if you are always having financial struggles, it can be due to a scarcity mindset program that was inserted during your childhood. Such as watching your parent(s) struggle, or in lack, or them spending money on drugs and alcohol, instead of buying food and paying the bills, and not buying you what you needed and wanted.

This creates a fearful and negative perception towards money early on in your childhood and becomes embedded in your subconscious. This will have you operating in a lack mentality as you get older, leading to intrusive thoughts in regards to money. It may also cause you to believe that money is the key to every problem and will make you feel better, when it will not. However, going within and doing some deep soul searching and healing, will help you fix your distorted perception and reality, and overcome your problems. And change your negative mentality and get you in alignment and in the flow for what is for you and what it is you are creating.

Until then, you will continue to loop and never have a healthy relationship with money, and you will continue to emotionally and impulsively spend money and create money blockages in your reality until you start to deprogram and align with the currency. So, it is best to get to the root of your problems in order to heal and build a solid foundation from the ground up. Because reconstruction often requires deconstruction or the dismantling of unstable foundations.

And the way to get to the root of your problems is through meditation, stillness, or reflection. Asking yourself questions and sitting still and quiet, allowing the answers to flow through you.

You will never really have to look outside yourself for answers when you have the fortitude to go within and allow the answers to come to you when facing obstacles and challenges.

Also, be aware that there are many distractions in the outer-world set up to disconnect and stop you from exploring and navigating your inner-world, so that you don't self-reflect, heal, and bring your visions into reality.

So sometimes you must shut the outer-world off and sit in solitude to discover the hidden powers and depths of yourself aka YOU-niverse and the workings of the outer-world/external world. And even though the external world may be chaotic (because the show/illusions must go on), remember that your internal landscape is your sanctuary. And the things outside of you appearing as chaos and challenges is for your internal growth (so that you can build your external landscape sanctuary, and still maintain your inner-peace no matter the chaos and storms happening outside of you).

So, take notes, and remember that you cannot change what is going on around or outside of you, until you heal and change what is going on within you. And as you heal and align internally, chaos dissipate externally because you are no longer battling internally within yourself, which changes how your outer-world respond to you. Because your internal state dictates how you perceive, interact with, and influence the world around you.

Outer-World

The world outside of you is called the outer-world aka the maya/matrix. The world of the collective consciousness-unconsciousness. It is where the systems are put in place to program and control the masses. These systems are systematic racism, man-made laws, economic system, education system, religion system, entertainment system and government system etc.

These systems are put in place to make your reality appear real (when they are really put in place to control and put fear in you). And make you feel like you are a part of something important. The outer-world makes you feel that if you are not a part of these systems or follow them then you are a menace to

society or a failure at life.

You have been programmed to believe that you must work

in their system to live and be somebody. When the animals you

see out in nature every day, for example, the squirrels and birds

do not pay bills or work for shelter or food, they also raise and

teach their own offspring(s) and are very resourceful.

They use the resources that the Divine has put here to care

for themselves. Just as we should be doing as well. However, we

cannot because the people that call themselves in charge take our

free resources and charge us for them and attach them to man-

made laws.

But people love the system and do not know how to

function without it. Then after working all their life, they realize

that they have wasted most of their time participating in the rat race, building someone else's dream instead of your own. They really do not know who they are as a spiritual being, having a human experience.

They never really got to know their inner-world. They were so focused on the outer-world, when the (B.I.B.L.E) basic information before leaving earth, mentioned, to be of the world but not in the world. But a lot of people missed the meaning of that.

So, they never got to do the things that their soul was yearning to do; doing this incarnation, which was to evolve their soul. And they wonder where that time went that passed them by so swiftly.

Now they are depressed and having a mid-life crisis, because their soul is crying out to them to do the things that they were called to do, but instead got lost in the outer-world.

These systems in the outer-world have distracted and trapped them and time is almost up, and they do not know who they truly are. They had to wear many masks in the outer-world to be a part of the so-called societal-norm. And they never really got to know their inner-world or complete the mission that brought them here.

And they never lived in their true essence. And the depression and misery kicks in, because they realize what huge mistakes they have made throughout life, by not using their time wisely. Instead of going inward and healing and tapping into their own gifts, creativity, and talents and pursuing and building their own dreams, that would have helped with their soul's evolution and purpose. They chose the outer-world for external validation instead of the road less-traveled (inner-world).

Natal Chart/Birth Chart

When you arrived in this earthly realm your parents were given a natal chart at the hospital you were born at. It's called a birth chart in astrology. However, the hospital you were born at undermined it as if it were just weight, measurements, hands, and footprints. These officials in high places know that there will be different waves of Starseed children, with unique spiritual gifts, that are specially sent; with a specific mission to help humanity and bring change to this earthly realm.

However, a birth chart is like a summary of the celestial positions in the sky at the time of your arrival to Earth. It shows how the stars were aligned, your placements of planets, houses, and your sun, moon, and rising sign.

Also, keep in mind these celestial bodies are energy. And these energies are within you. And depending on other factors such as degrees, angles, conjunctions, trines, stelliums, houses, etc, and the zodiac signs and their position within the planets is the makeup of who you are.

For example, the Sun could have been in Virgo in the 6th house at 22.2 degrees, Moon in Capricorn in the 9th house at 22.3 degrees, Venus in Pisces in the 12th house at 22.4 degrees, etc.

Also, it's of great importance and meticulous in how you read and study your chart. But knowing your birth chart is essential because it's your blueprint to this life and what lessons you came here to learn while you are here attending Earth school.

It is your true story and what your soul came here to do. It will help you discover your purpose and your soul mission. It also reveal things from your past life experiences and the things you overcame or went through. As well as the kind of experiences you will have while you are here.

Whether that will be in your childhood or adulthood. And some of it will not be pleasant. But it is for your soul's evolution.

But if you are aware of your birth chart it can be used as a tool to help you with the navigation your life. So, you do not repeat the same lessons and feel helpless and stuck on the hamster wheel while you are here. And feeling like you are a victim, and life is hard and unbearable.

In addition, your birth chart shows you your personality type, passions, interests, characteristics, motivations, desires, strengths, weaknesses, gifts, and the types of relationships you will attract or experience etc.

Also, your north-node shows the direction you are headed or supposed to be headed in this lifetime, and your south-node shows past life experiences and some of the things that came

along with you in this lifetime. And what you might need to

release this lifetime.

To sum it up, astrology is just a divination tool to help you

get to know more about who you are as a spiritual being having a

human experience. And you can calculate your birth chart online

for free using a birth chart calculator. So, use this information

wisely.

And it's probably not a good idea to share your information

with just any and everybody. Cause people can use certain things

in your chart to derail, control and manipulate you.

Realms/Dimensions/Timelines

There are many realms, dimensions and timelines of existence. Which one you experience largely depends on your vibrational frequency and whether you're in a physical or non-physical state.

And for those that think this Earthly realm is a struggle or horrible, understand that there are even lower realms and planes of existence, some of which intertwine with this one and others that are separate from it.

And when it comes to timelines, your vibration and thought forms will determine which one you're on or tuned into, and this will reflect in your outer-world.

So, if you are tuning into negative energies and low frequencies and vibrations that are put in place to keep the masses under a spell and on autopilot. Then that will be the timeline reflected in your world, the collective timeline.

But if your third eye and crown chakras are activated, and your thought-forms are of high vibrations, aligning you with all positive, high vibrational frequencies, and energies, then you'll be spiritually and mentally placed in a higher timeline that differ from the masses.

And you won't be affected by the negative energies projected from the outer-world and others, because they'll simply cease to exist in your state of existence or consciousness.

However, should you encounter these past negative energies, it's the Divine testing your progression to see if you are maintaining your own vibration and timeline, or if you'll fold under pressure.

So, basically, you'll only experience people, places, or things that are a vibrational match.

For instance, you could walk past someone you know, and they might not even see or recognize you because you are vibrating on a higher timeline and in a different dimension that they're not tapped into. Like Jesus said, " In my Father's Kingdom there are many mansions," in John 14:2. Meaning, there are many dimensions, timelines, and realms.

Now, in this physical realm called Earth, or the third default dimension, where many souls come to learn lessons and complete missions, some unfortunately get trapped. They become so caught up in the experiences and illusions that they forget why they're here and who they truly are. As a result, they begin to spiral down instead of spiraling up and ascending to higher consciousness where higher dimensions exist.

The genetically modified food and vaccination shots they received upon arriving here, coupled with intense programming, contributes to them becoming lost and trapped in lower dimensions. Additionally, their spiritual centers, or chakras, have been shut down.

So, the path forward often requires a spiritual awakening or the activation of their chakras, enabling them to enter higher states of consciousness and awareness. However, they must first awaken to themselves (Get Off AutoPilot), and to the information that lies dormant within them.

But so much has transpired while being here; so much suffering and so many challenges, obstacles, and distractions makes it difficult for these souls to awaken and tap into the detailed files that are within them.

So, they're unable to receive downloads or tap into their intuition, which would help them navigate this realm effectively and efficiently. But once they awaken, come into awareness, and begin to self-discover, they can choose to ascend and master this realm.

And once these souls have a spiritual awakening, and begin to heal their past, and master their lessons, and break free from karmic cycles, and fulfill their divine mission, they are then able to consciously transition to other dimensions and realms that exist simultaneously, with this 3D default reality, and transcend its limitations and boundaries.

<u>Chakras</u>

There are seven main chakras in your body. It's said that a person have a total of one hundred and fourteen chakras. Chakra's look like wheels or spinning disks. They are known as spiritual centers or energy centers that work as transformers that control the energy within your body, when they are activated and spinning.

But the main seven chakras are the root, sacral, solar plexus, heart, throat, third eye, and crown. These are the seven that are most talked about and are aligned from the base of your spine to the crown of your head. Which you may know as the 33 vertebrae, the kundalini rising/path, Christ path, serpent energy, or the biblical term "Jacob's ladder. However, it's all the same motion, energy rising from the base of your spine to the crown of your head, which is an illustration of the ascension process to

Christ Consciousness.

These chakra's balance the spiritual body, the mental and

your emotional and physical health, or mind, body, and spirit.

Each of these chakras will spin when activated which in return will

create a vortex of energy that draws in your universal life force.

And emits energy that carries detailed information or energy with

intentions.

For example, when the crown chakra is activated and

balanced you will have clarity, mental sharpness, a sense of

purpose and direct contact with your higher self, the spiritual

realm, other realms, and the Divine. This specific chakra is linked

to your brain and nervous system. And located at the top of your

head within your cerebral cortex.

And this chakra is associated with the color violet or light purple. But when it is blocked or shut off you have no information from the source or any other higher intelligence. And you are disconnected from your mind, body and spirit.

Some things that block off your crown chakra are psychological trauma or the inability to cope with emotional stress, and feelings of fear, shame, or guilt. Ways to unblock this chakra is healing and finding healthy coping mechanisms to deal with emotional wreckage and trauma. Also, certain crystals, meditation, breathing exercises, yoga, mantras or mudras will unblock this chakra.

Also, when your throat chakra's is activated and balanced it is easy for you to assert your beliefs and truth unapologetically. This chakra is in the center of your neck, near the thyroid gland

and larynx at the base of your throat. And associated with the color blue.

But if it is blocked or shut down you do not have this ability to express yourself with confidence. You fear your own voice and the ridicule and judgement from others. Things that block or shut down your throat chakra is childhood trauma, being yelled at by a parent or caregiver, or being told to shut-up by others, or physical and emotional abuse.

Some of the way to unblock this chakra is to heal those traumas by speaking your truth to those that hurt you or journaling, neck stretches, yoga poses, throat crystals, meditation, mantras, and mudras or wearing the color blue.

Lastly, the heart chakra is associated with the color green and located in the middle of your chest. When your heart chakra is activated and balanced, you will self-love and open yourself up to love. You are compassionate towards others.

You know how to set healthy boundaries with others. You have and show empathy towards others. But when it is blocked or shut off you repel love, you are self-loathing and are not considerate of others' feelings or emotions.

You have a heightened need for love, acceptance, and validation from others. You have a hard time trusting and forgiving others. You feel some form of fear, shame or guilt. And you put yourself at risk for heart and lung complications and high blood pressure.

Things that block your heart chakra are from some form of heart break or loss, anger, and bitterness block your heart chakra. Childhood trauma like abandonment or betrayal blocks your heart chakra.

And emotional and physical abuse blocks your heart chakra. But ways to heal and unblock this chakra is releasing negativity, self-love, self-care, self-acceptance, and self-validation.

Be authentic with yourself and others. Be forgiving towards yourself and others. Show gratitude and compassion towards yourself and others. Inner-child healing and shadow work can also unblock your heart chakra.

Also, just as mentioned above, yoga, meditation, breath work, mantras, mudras, and crystals can unblock your heart chakra.

In conclusion, these are just three of the seven main chakras I have mentioned. It is best to do your due diligence and research and study these chakras on your own. So, your mind, body, and spirit can be aligned as one.

Crystals

Crystals have many powers, benefits, and healing abilities that can assist your mind, body, and soul. Our ancestors used crystals and knew the healing abilities and powers they possess. They were in tune with nature and knew crystals held their own energy, frequency, and vibration.

And since we are energy/spiritual beings and crystals have an energy of their own, we can transfer energy with these crystals or use them to balance ourselves or different parts of our body just by wearing them, carrying them, or placing them on a certain part of our body.

Which in return will help you with emotional, spiritual, or physical healing. Or repel negative energies that are not in alignment with the high vibration frequencies you exude. For example, wearing or carrying a black tourmaline can repel negative forces that are trying to attack you in some way shape or form.

Furthermore, it is a good idea to research and study and be knowledgeable with different crystals and see how they can benefit you along your journey and to know how to differentiate the real crystals from the fake crystals.

Also, some people that are ignorant will tell you that tapping into certain spiritual practices is ungodly and evil. And the others will demonize it, just like anything else that can help you, they demonize it. But the bible mentions that the New Jerusalem's wall being made of Jasper and other precious stones. And how Aaron's breastplate, had an Amethyst which is considered a crystal and a gemstone. But moving along, there are so many crystals for love, protection, clarity, grounding, and many other things like balancing or activating your chakras. So, get familiar with the different ones and use them in your everyday life to promote the wellness of your spiritual human experience.

In addition, wearing or carrying your birthstone(s) or zodiac stone(s) can be beneficial as well. Because they are unique and tailor-made to you as an individual and will help enhance or expand you in certain areas of your life that needs improvement.

Or help you overcome the things you struggle or battle with, just the same as crystals can do as well. Crystals and gemstones are different but similar in some ways. But they both can have a positive impact on your life if you choose to utilize them.

Word Alchemy

The English language is witchcraft, a cursing, spellbound, spirit binding, spellcasting language. That is why you had S-P-E-L-L-I-N-G class in elementary and was taught cursive (curses) in your early development stages. They were creating the "Hive Mind" (the Collective Conscious-Unconsciousness) putting curses on you to put you to sleep and you were being unconsciously programmed to cast spells on yourself and others, while following the same collective conscious-unconsciousness, detrimental programs that were and are scripting your reality, the one they created and creating for you, the "Hive Mind" (the Collective Conscious-Unconsciousness) reality. Therefore, you became a participant in your own imprisonment.

And you have been using certain words without knowing that you are casting spells on yourself. Like when you say, "I'm broke," you are speaking lack over your life. Or when you say, "I can't wait for the weekend, what you are really saying is you can't wait to be weaken.

Or the slang the youth use, I'm dead, I'm weak, you killing me, or you sick. These negative words can lead to negative outcomes. Because they are unconsciously speaking ill towards themselves and others. And the tongue is powerful, it can speak life or death.

Furthermore, words that you thought were good but held a different energy and vibration such as "bless" is broken down to b-less. Or to say you are black, to b-lack (be in lack) or meaning wicked, unlucky, bad, or malicious.

And when you say "good morning" you are telling someone to be good in their mourning. Or words that you say after being thanked for something by saying you're welcome (Wel-Come) to someone can invite unwelcome energies or spirits into your energy field or life.

So, try saying be bliss or you are bliss or have a blissful day instead of a bless day. Or say you are original, organic, or indigenous instead of black. And instead of saying good morning you can say "Supreme or Rich Rising or Grand Rising". Also, instead of saying you're welcome say no problem or Wealth come.

You must start to be conscious of the things you say. Start speaking life over yourself and others, and not words that can be detrimental to the psyche or your well-being. Start to use words that empower you and that are transformative by speaking positive affirmations over your life to affirm things you want to bring into reality and not words that keep you locked in loops are suffering.

Once you learn to replace words and phrases that limit and hinder you with those that inspire and uplift, you'll gain the ability to transform your life and embrace a more positive outlook on life.

In summary, stop using low vibrational frequency words that impact your life in a negative manner. Know that words hold energy and have a vibrational frequency and when you are not conscious of the words you speak or read, they can have a negative effect on your well-being.

Once you know this you can use words to improve and transform your life and uplift your spirit. You can also begin to manifest your dreams into reality. You can speak things into existence just by speaking life over yourself, situations, and circumstances.

If you constantly speaking life, affirmations, and your dreams out to the universe, they will not come back void. But you must remain steadfast and persevere no matter the hardships and challenges you go through.

And sometimes things fall apart for new things to emerge. So, no matter what always remain positive and continue to speak and think positive no matter what difficulties you face. Know that all challenges is an opportunity for growth. And everything is happening and aligning in your favor. And do not underestimate the power and the impact that words can have whether that be positive or negative. Everything is energy, frequencies, and vibrations.

YOUR GIFTS AND POWER LIES WITHIN YOU-THEY HAVE ALWAYS BEEN WITHIN YOU-WAITING FOR YOU TO TAP INTO THEM.

-GODDESS RAVIN NICOLE

www.ingramcontent.com/pod-product-compliance
Lightning Source LLC
LaVergne TN
LVHW051152080426
835508LV00021B/2594